A 3-minute forever book

EAT YOUR PEAS®

for the Holidays

By Cheryl Karpen
Gently Spoken Communications

A gift for

Gwen

from

Kimberly

Merry Christmas
2007!

This is an amazing time of year...
the **lights**
the lists
the laughter
and
the longing
for meaning in our lives.

Which brings me to you
and all the amazing ways
you
give meaning and *joy* to my life.

May this little book
make you
smile,
make you
glad
and remind you
how much you mean to me.

It's true.
Some gifts
are
`priceless.`

Oh starry, starry night, grant my friend a wish tonight.

Let this time of year
inspire us to celebrate
life's simplest joys

a
tender
hug

a
prayer
uplifted

a
random act
of
kindness

May all the

razzle dazzle

of the season
never blind us to the
true meaning of these days.

Peas
on
earth.

Goodwill to everyone.

Let's rejoice
in
celebration
and
make angels
in the snow...
or
sand!

The Holidays

A time for:

hot cocoa

twinkling lights

gingerbread cookies

candy canes

new p.j.s

apple pie a la mode

crackling fires

Sure ways to get in the spirit:
Taste
one of everything.
Sing
at the top of your lungs.
Give
from the bottom of your heart.
Speak
hope where it's needed most.

When decking the halls,
remember to...
decorate,
recuperate,
decorate,
recuperate!

Always keep
mistletoe
close at hand.

You'll never know when you
might need it!

At the first sign of feeling
overwhelmed, underfunded,
or up a chimney
call me
and I will remind you
why we go through this
every year.

No matter
the distance between us,
I promise to be
just a phone call
or smile away.

With you in my life,
it's a

Wonderful life!

Merry, merry, merry...

Whenever
I think of you,
I feel
merrier!

I think you've been
very good
this year.

No lumps of coal
for you...

With the holidays,
comes the promise of
a new year.

May yours be the best one yet.

Savor
the
celebration
and
remember to always

Eat Your Peas!

Why Peas?

She was a vibrant, dazzling young woman with a promising future.
Yet, at sixteen, her world felt sad and hopeless.

I was living over 1800 miles away and wanted to let this very special young person in my life know I would be there for her across the miles and through the darkness. I wanted her to know she could call me any time, at any hour, and I would be there for her. And I wanted to give her a piece of my heart she could take with her anywhere—a reminder she was loved.

Really loved.

Her name is Maddy and she was the inspiration for my first PEAS book, **Eat Your Peas for Young Adults**. At the very beginning of her book I made a place to write in my phone number so she knew I was serious about being available. And right beside the phone number I put my promise to listen—really listen—whenever that call came.

Soon after the book was published, people began to ask me if I had the same promise and affirmation for adults. I realized it isn't just young people who need to be reminded how truly special they are. **We all do.**

Today Maddy is thriving and giving hope to others in her life.
If someone has given you this book, it means you are pretty special
to them and they wanted to let you know. Take it to heart.

Believe it, and remind yourself often.

Wishing you peas and plenty of joy,

Cheryl Karpen

P.S. If you are wondering why I named the collection, Eat Your Peas...it's my way of saying, "Stay healthy. I love and cherish you. I want you to live **forever!**"

A portion of the profits from the
Eat Your Peas Collection
will benefit empowerment programs
for youth and adults.

Special thanks to...

Artist, **Sandy Fougner** and editor, **Suzanne Foust**
for bringing so much spirit and joy
to the Eat Your Peas Collection.
What talent you behold!

To my husband, **Mark**, for
re-creating the holidays on a chilly
and gray April afternoon.
Festive music filled the air,
bright and shiny decorations were hung,
and the inspiration (and fun!) began.

And lastly, to my
family and the many friends
that have made my holidays
such a treasure of love and inspiration.

You are cherished.

~CK

About the author

"Eat Your Peas"

A self-proclaimed dreamer, Cheryl
spends her time imagining and creating
between the historic river town of Anoka, Minnesota
and the seaside village of Islamorada, Florida.

An effervescent speaker, Cheryl brings inspiration,
insight, and humor to corporations,
professional organizations and churches.
Learn more about her at: www.cherylkarpen.com

About the illustrator

Sandy Fougner artfully weaves
a love for design, illustration and
interiors with being a wife
and mother of three sons.

Other books by Cheryl Karpen

The Eat Your Peas Collection™

is now available in the following titles:

Daughters   Girlfriends
Sons   Someone Special
Mothers   Birthdays
Fathers   New Moms
Sisters   Tough Times
Grandkids   Sweethearts
Grandparents   Me
     Teens

New titles are SPROUTING up all the time!

Heart and Soul Collection

To Let You Know I Care
Hope for a Hurting Heart
Can We Try Again? Finding a way back to love

To view a complete collection, visit us on-line at **www.eatyourpeas.com**

Eat Your Peas® for Holidays

For more information or to locate a store near you, contact:
Gently Spoken
PO Box 245
Anoka, MN 55303

Toll-free 1-877-224-7886 or visit us on-line at
www.eatyourpeas.com